THE LIFE CYCLE OF A Cat

By Colleen Sexton

BELLWETHER MEDIA · MINNEAPOLIS, MN

BLASTOFF! READERS 3

Note to Librarians, Teachers, and Parents:

Blastoff! Readers are carefully developed by literacy experts and combine standards-based content with developmentally appropriate text.

Level 1 provides the most support through repetition of high-frequency words, light text, predictable sentence patterns, and strong visual support.

Level 2 offers early readers a bit more challenge through varied simple sentences, increased text load, and less repetition of high-frequency words.

Level 3 advances early-fluent readers toward fluency through increased text and concept load, less reliance on visuals, longer sentences, and more literary language.

Level 4 builds reading stamina by providing more text per page, increased use of punctuation, greater variation in sentence patterns, and increasingly challenging vocabulary.

Level 5 encourages children to move from "learning to read" to "reading to learn" by providing even more text, varied writing styles, and less familiar topics.

Whichever book is right for your reader, Blastoff! Readers are the perfect books to build confidence and encourage a love of reading that will last a lifetime!

This edition first published in 2011 by Bellwether Media, Inc.

No part of this publication may be reproduced in whole or in part without written permission of the publisher. For information regarding permission, write to Bellwether Media, Inc., Attention: Permissions Department, 5357 Penn Avenue South, Minneapolis, MN 55419.

Library of Congress Cataloging-in-Publication Data
Sexton, Colleen A., 1967–
  The life cycle of a cat / by Colleen Sexton.
    p. cm. — (Blastoff! readers. Life cycles)
  Summary: "Developed by literacy experts for students in grades kindergarten through three, this book follows cats as they transform from birth to adult. Through leveled text and related images, young readers will watch these creatures grow through every stage of life"–Provided by publisher.
  Includes bibliographical references and index.
  ISBN 978-1-60014-449-3 (hardcover : alk. paper)
  1. Cats–Life cycles–Juvenile literature. I. Title.
  SF445.7.S492 2010
  636.8–dc22   2010000704

Printed in the United States of America, North Mankato, MN.
080110   1162

Contents

Cats are the most popular pets on the planet. More than 600 million cats live in homes around the world!

There are more than 30 cat **breeds**. They come in many sizes and colors. They can have short fur or long fur.

All cats grow and change in stages.
The stages of a cat's **life cycle** are
birth, kitten, and adult.

birth

kitten

adult

A female cat gives birth to a kitten. The kitten is part of a **litter**. Most litters have three to five kittens.

The mother licks the kitten's wet fur.
The kitten begins to breathe.

The kitten cannot hear or open its eyes. It snuggles close to its mother to keep warm.

The kitten is hungry. It drinks milk from its mother.

The kitten sleeps when
it is not eating. Sleeping
helps it grow.

The kitten can see and hear when it is two weeks old. It learns how to **groom** its soft fur.

The kitten has sharp teeth when it is four weeks old. It eats solid food and drinks fresh water.

The kitten's legs are strong when it is six weeks old. The kitten explores. It runs from place to place.

The kitten plays with toys. It jumps and tumbles.
It wrestles with its brothers and sisters.

The kitten stays with its mother until it is about eight weeks old. Then it goes to a new home.

The kitten grows bigger and stronger every day. It can jump high. It uses its sharp claws to climb.

The kitten is an adult when it is one year old. It is all grown up!

Adult cats can have kittens. A male
cat and a female cat **mate**.

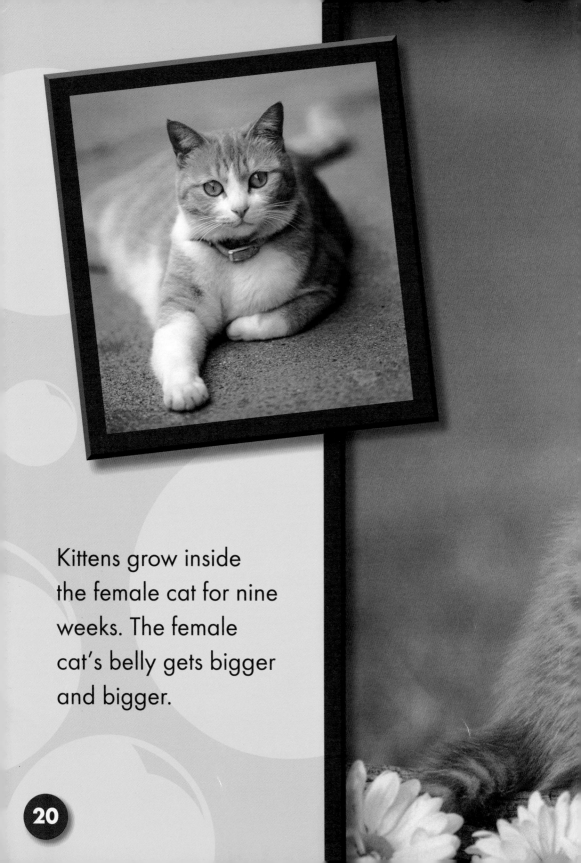

Kittens grow inside
the female cat for nine
weeks. The female
cat's belly gets bigger
and bigger.

The female cat gives birth to a litter. Each tiny kitten is the start of a new life cycle!

Glossary

breeds—different kinds of cats that have the same body features; some of the most popular cat breeds are Persian, Maine Coon, Siamese, Abyssinian, and Ragdoll; many cats are a mix of breeds.

groom—to wash away dirt; cats use their rough tongues to groom their fur.

life cycle—the stages of life of an animal; a life cycle includes being born, growing up, having young, and dying.

litter—a group of animals born at the same time to one mother; a cat litter can have one to nine kittens; most litters have three to five kittens.

mate—to join together to produce young

To Learn More

AT THE LIBRARY

Magloff, Lisa. *Kitten*. New York, N.Y.: DK Publishing, 2005.

Meyers, Susan. *Kittens! Kittens! Kittens!* New York, N.Y.: Abram's Books for Young Readers, 2007.

Sexton, Colleen. *Kittens*. Minneapolis, Minn.: Bellwether Media, 2008.

ON THE WEB

Learning more about life cycles is as easy as 1, 2, 3.

1. Go to www.factsurfer.com.

2. Enter "life cycles" into the search box.

3. Click the "Surf" button and you will see a list of related Web sites.

With factsurfer.com, finding more information is just a click away.

Index

The images in this book are reproduced through the courtesy of: Lee O'Dell, front cover; Juniors Bildarchiv/Age Fotostock, front cover (birth), pp. 6 (birth), 16; Gregor Kervina, front cover (kitten), pp. 6 (kitten), 14; Henk Bentlage, front cover (adult); Imagesource/Photolibrary, pp. 4-5; David Fowler, p. 5 (small); Cristi Bastian, p. 6 (adult); M. Wegler Katzengeburt/Juniors Bildarchiv, pp. 7, 9, 15; Jane Burton/naturepl.com, p. 8; Jean Michel Labat/Ardea, pp. 10-11; Tatjana Strelkova, p. 11 (small); Petra Wegner/Alamy, p. 12; Juan Martinez, p. 13; Juniors Bildarchiv/Age Fotostock, p. 17; Daniel Rajszczak, p. 18; Juniors Bildarchiv, p. 19; Shuji Aizawa & Kyoko Aizawa/Photolibrary, p. 20 (small); Gary Randall/KimballStock, pp. 20-21.